THE LANDS OF OZ
GILLIKIN COUNTRY
WINKIE COUNTRY
MUNCHKINLAND
QUADLING COUNTRY
INVISIBLE COUNTRY
EMERALD CITY
UPPER UPLANDS
PUMPERDINK HILLS
SHIZ
LAUGHING WILLOWS
REERA
GILLIKENNY
SAPPHIRE CITY
LAKE ORIZON
TULIP MOUNTAINS
FOREST OF GUGU
SOUP SEA
TURN TOWN
GILLIKIN MOUNTAINS
BACK WOODS
INLAND SEA
MURKY MANSION
BLANKENBERG
HIDDEN VALLEY
WINKIE PEAKS
WINKIE PALACE
DANGEROUS PASSAGE
REGALIA
CRYSTAL CAVERNS
BANDIT CAVE
POPPY FIELDS
FILKIN FOLLY
YOOP
NIKIDIK TOWERS
DARK FOREST
PERHAPS
CAVE CITY
GOVERNOR'S MANSION
GREAT GILLIKIN FOREST
SHUTTER TOWN
MOUNT MUNCH
GILLIKIN RIVER
SQUEE-GEE VILLE
FIGHTING TREES
LONESOME MOUND
WEIRD WOODS
ROLLING LANDS
UGU
MUNCHKIN VILLAGE
GORGBAS GARDEN
PATCH
MISTY VALLEY
FISKIN TOWN
BLUE FOREST
MUNCHKIN RIVER
CRYSTAL CITY
FLAT MOUNTAINS
WINKIE WOODS
GREAT WINKIE RIVER
RUDDERBURY HILLOCK
BEAR TOWERS
SQUIRREL KINGDOM
CRYSTAL SWAMP
KING KREWL KINGDOM
HAMMERHEADS DWELL
HOLKUM HILLS
POINTY PEAKS
HERKU
TRICK RIVER
THE CURIOUS COPSE
CHIMNEYVILLE
JELLYTOP MOUNTAIN
WORRIED WOODS
KIAMO KO
QUADLING RIVER
MURKY MARSH
RUBY CAVERNS
BAFFLEBURG
LAND OF THE BARONS
EUREKA FOREST
STRANGE FOREST
UTENSIA
LOLLIPOP VILLAGE
KINGDOM OF BUNNYBURY
RED TOPS MOUNTAINS
TWINLET TOWN
SCARE CITY
RUDDERBURY
QUADLING KEEP

# THE FACES & PLACES OF OZ

DEYST.

*An Imprint of* WILLIAM MORROW

PART I

# Munchkinland

WELCOME TO
MUNCHKINLAND

UNCHKINLAND IS a small village that lies in the eastern plains of Oz and is home to the Munchkins. The town is surrounded by a sea of tulips and populated with houses built close together and covered in thatched roofing of brightly colored straw. In the center of the village is a town square for village functions.

The Munchkins are easily identifiable by their curly red hair. It's here in their humble village that the story of Elphaba Thropp begins . . .

BEWARE
THE
GREEN

ELPHABA THROPP

**"I don't cause commotions.
I am one."**

***—Elphaba Thropp***

ELDEST DAUGHTER OF GOVERNOR THROPP, THE GOVERNOR OF Munchkinland, Elphaba Thropp stood out from the moment she was born. Scorned by her father for her green skin, Elphaba finds solace in her relationships with her younger sister, Nessarose, and her nanny, Dulcibear.

But her green skin is only one of Elphaba's unique traits. She was also born with magical abilities; however, her gift is tied to her emotions, and she struggles to control them. Still, her skill is impressive enough to grant her a personal invitation to the illustrious Shiz University. It's there that she learns to harness her emotions, which sets her on a path that intertwines her destiny with the Wizard, and all of Oz.

THE Story OF OZ
& THE WONDERFUL WIZARD

*Elphaba Thropp*

NESSAROSE THROPP

**"Mother's jeweled shoes? Thank you! Thank you so much! I love them."**

***—Nessarose Thropp***

DOTED ON BY HER FATHER AND FIERCELY PROTECTED BY HER older sister, Nessarose "Nessa" Thropp is often described as tragically beautiful. Her inability to walk was caused by her mother consuming milk flowers throughout pregnancy, in order to prevent Nessarose from having green skin like Elphaba.

Despite losing her mother during childbirth, Nessarose maintains a positive attitude. She is excited for a new life at Shiz University, where she meets fellow Munchkin Boq Woodsman, a love interest that leads to lasting consequences for both.

BOQ WOODSMAN

**"I'm Boq.**
**From Munchkinland."**
***—Boq Woodsman***

SHORT IN STATURE BUT ALTRUISTIC IN NATURE, BOQ IS A kind-hearted Munchkin with a mop of curly red hair.

Along with Elphaba and Nessarose, Boq also meets the popular Glinda Upland for whom he develops a crush. But it's Glinda's facilitation of an evening with Nessarose at the Ozdust Ballroom that changes the course of his life forever . . .

Governor
Thropp's House

# Life in Munchkinland

With a grand town center, the citizens of Munchkinland celebrate their agrarian roots through harvest festivals and other community projects throughout the year, including their A-maze-ifying Cornfield Maze, community gardens, and their Tulip Fair.

MUNCHKINLAND'S
FAMOUS
Tulip Fair

COMMENCING THIS LEAF FALL
SEASON,
EVERY EARLY
PLACE TO ADMIRE SUCH
MUNCHKINLAND BECOMES THE
CONTAIN. THIS JOYOUS BLANKET OF
COLORFUL FLOWER FIELDS AS THE EYE CAN
COLOR SEEMS TO BE THE HERALD OF THE NEW SEASON AHEAD, OF NEW LIFE AND NEW THINGS TO WEL-
COME THE DAY. PEOPLE FROM ALL OVER OZ TRAVEL TO MUNCHKINLAND TO ADMIRE THE ENORMOUS
FIELDS OF WILDLY COLORFUL TULIPS THAT SWAY IN THE SOFT BREEZES OF THE RURAL COUNTRY.
MUNCHKINLAND'S FAMOUS
TulipFair
NO ONE KNOW
TULIP ORIGINAT-
ACADEMIC STUD-
THE TULIP IS AN
BE FOUND ANY-
DESERT PLANES JUST
ERN PART OF MUNCHKIN
WHERE THE
ED BUT
IES SUG-
GEST THAT
ORIGINAL FLOWER OF MUNCHKINLAND AND NOT TO
WHERE ELSE. GROWING IN ITS ANCIENT FORM ON THE
NEAR THE BORDER OF THE DEADLY DESERT IN THE EAST-
COUNTRY, THE TULIP WAS A SIGN OF LIFE NEAR THAT FATAL
SAND OCEAN. ITS BEAUTY BECAME A SIGN OF HOPE AND AN EMBLEM OR BEACON OF ALL THAT IS
LOVELY AND WELCOMING IN MUNCHKIN COUNTRY, ONE OF THE FRIENDLIEST REGIONS IN OZ.
THE TULIP FAIR THEN HAS ITS ROOTS IN THE FURTHEST HISTORY OF MUNCHKINLAND. WHILE THE COUN-
TRY MAY BE BEST KNOWN NOW AS THE BREADBASKET OF OZ, MUNCHKINS KNOW THAT THE LAND
UPON WHICH THEY LIVE IS THE GARDEN OF THIS WONDEROUS LAND.
AT THE TULIP FAIR, YOU CAN OBTAIN BULBS FOR NEXT SEASON'S PLANTINGS. THERE ARE SWEETS IN
THE SHAPES OF TULIPS ~ WITH ALL THE
THE
COLORS ~ AS WELL
FLAVORS OF
AS TALKS
AND TULIPS.
ON THE SIXTH FULL MOON

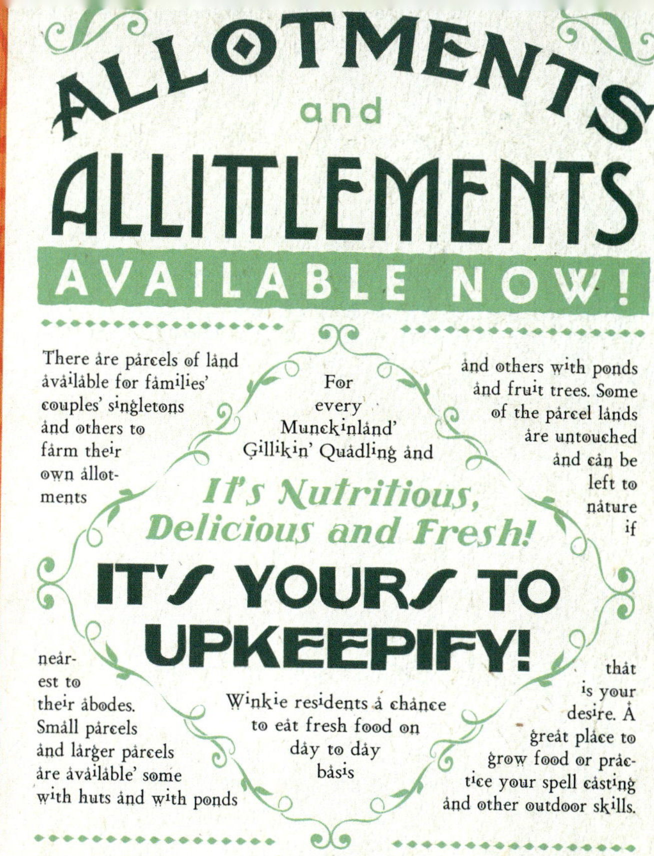
ALLOTMENTS
and
ALLITTLEMENTS
AVAILABLE NOW!
There are parcels of land available for families' couples' singletons and others to farm their own allot-ments
For every Munckinland' Gillikin' Quadling and
and others with ponds and fruit trees. Some of the parcel lands are untouched and can be left to nature if
It's Nutritious, Delicious and Fresh!
IT'S YOURS TO UPKEEPIFY!
near-est to their abodes. Small parcels and larger parcels are available' some with huts and with ponds
Winkie residents a chance to eat fresh food on day to day basis
that is your desire. A great place to grow food or prac-tice your spell casting and other outdoor skills.
THE PERFECTEST
MUNCHKINLAND LIFESTYLE!
The allotments are available on a fair basis of need and location. An inter-view may or may not be required. Your allotment will be given to you and can be made heritable if that is your request.
Get a Lot or a Little Today!

INITIALIZATION OF THE
YELLOW
BRICK ROAD
CONSTRUCTIVATION PROJECT
The Yellow Brick road is destined to level up all the transport needs of the average Ozian, hastening travel and lowering times of transport with considerable ease and speed.
and one which is bringing the promise of important communicative and regenerătative projects in all regions.
The YBR is a new high speed road surface being built from all corners of Oz to serve all corners of Oz, from the Emerald City at its heart to the outskirts and outlying areas where Ozians may be living out of touch with each other.
Major civil engineering works are now underway having contracted into the supply chain and including many active sites between The Emerald City and other centres of metropolitan life such as Scare
The new road, being built with extra help from the Gale Force army, will link Oz's biggest cities with

KEEP
MUNCHKINLAND
CLEAN!
ONLY YOU CAN PREVENT LITTER IN OZ'S BREADBASKET COUNTRY
KEEP YOUR HANDKERCHIEFS IN YOUR POCKETS
DO NOT CHEW FOR RECREATIONAL PURPOSES
LEAVE ITEMS AT HOME FOR INCINERATION
DON'T DROP OBJECTS WITHOUT THINKING
Munchkin Country is one of Oz's prettiest and cleaniest
areas. Do not leave books, food remains, wrappers or papers as if
someone else will clean them up. They won't magically disappear! The
notion of anything being disposable is fanciful thinking. Munchkinland is your home -
keep it tidy, sweet and pretty by being thoughtful and considerate in everything you do.
THE WIZARD HAS DEEMED MUNCHKINLAND IS YOURS TO ENJOY!
ENJOY IT CLEANLY!

PART 2

# Shiz University

# WELCOME TO SHIZ UNIVERSITY

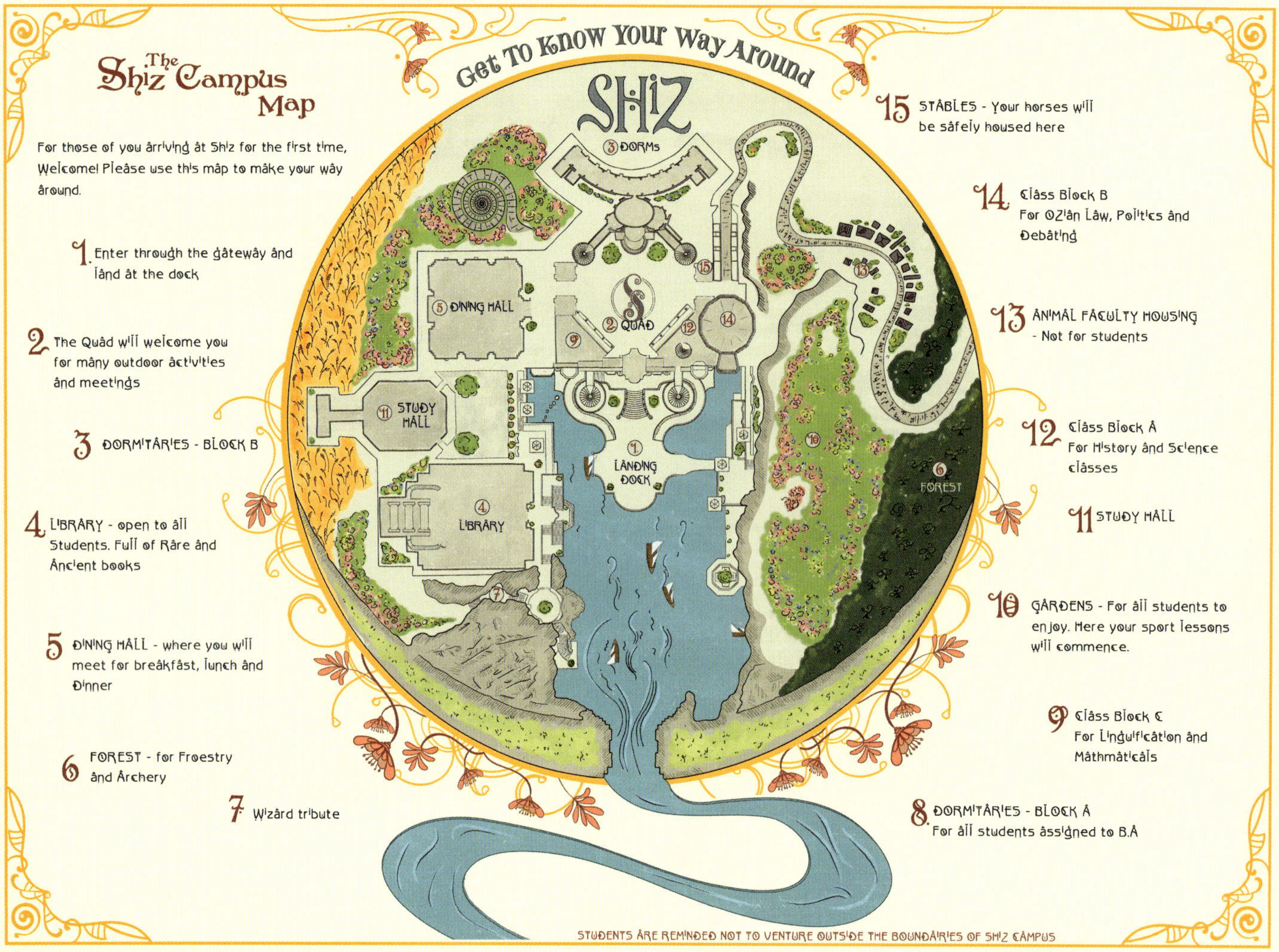
The Shiz Campus Map
For those of you arriving at Shiz for the first time, Welcome! Please use this map to make your way around.
1. Enter through the gateway and land at the dock
2. The Quad will welcome you for many outdoor activities and meetings
3 DORMITARIES - BLOCK B
4 LIBRARY - open to all Students. Full of Rare and Ancient books
5 DINING HALL - where you will meet for breakfast, lunch and Dinner
6 FOREST - for Froestry and Archery
7 Wizard tribute
Get To Know Your Way Around
SHIZ
3 DORMS
5 DINING HALL
2 QUAD
11 STUDY HALL
1 LANDING DOCK
4 LIBRARY
6 FOREST
15 STABLES - Your horses will be safely housed here
14 Class Block B For Ozian Law, Politics and Debating
13 ANIMAL FACULTY HOUSING - Not for students
12 Class Block A For History and Science classes
11 STUDY HALL
10 GARDENS - For all students to enjoy. Here your sport lessons will commence.
9 Class Block C For Linguification and Mathmaticals
8 DORMITARIES - BLOCK A For all students assigned to B.A
STUDENTS ARE REMINDED NOT TO VENTURE OUTSIDE THE BOUNDARIES OF SHIZ CAMPUS

OUR WONDERFUL
WIZARD OF OZ

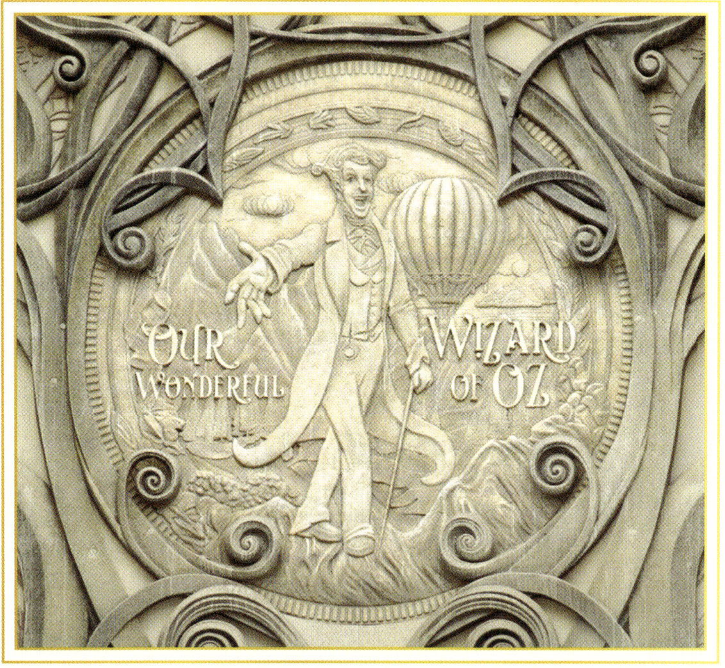

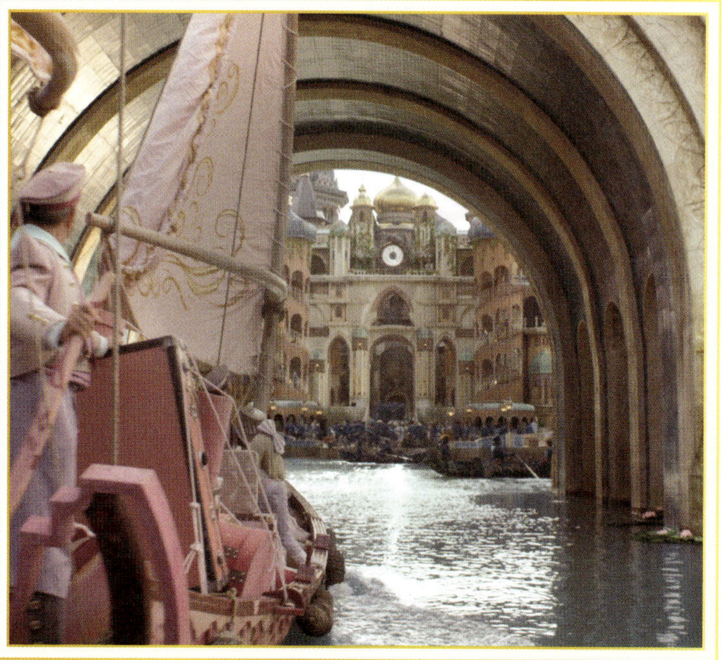

ILLUSTRIOUS SHIZ UNIVERSITY stands nobly in the northern plains of Oz. This waterfront university is home to Oz's finest minds, from its students to its faculty. From agriculture to history, the university attracts those from all over Oz who desire to learn.

It's here that Elphaba and Nessarose meet fellow students Glinda, Boq, and Fiyero, and where Elphaba is taken under the wing of the famed sorceress Madame Morrible, who helps hone her innate magical abilities.

Once a bastion of free thought among people and animals alike, Shiz has experienced changes over the years. In fact, Elphaba and her classmates witness the removal of Doctor Dillamond after it's announced that animals are no longer allowed to teach at Shiz.

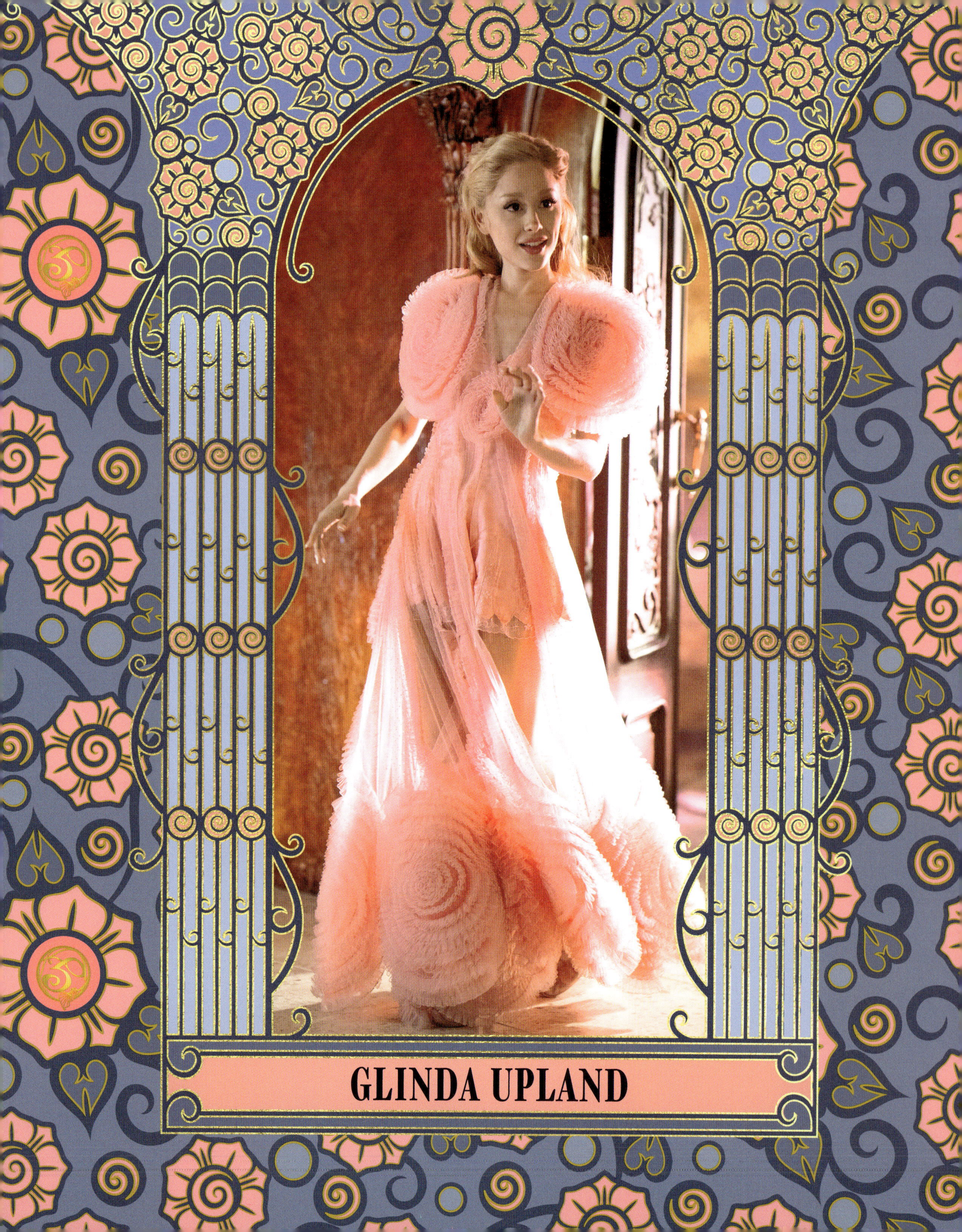
GLINDA UPLAND

**"I believe that strangers are just people I've never met."**

***—Glinda Upland***

Glinda Upland (of the Upper Uplands) dreams of becoming a sorceress and attends Shiz hoping to study magic at the hand of the great Madame Morrible. Thanks to her wit, charm, and absolutely enviable personal style, she quickly becomes the most popular student on campus, winning the adoration of fellow students Pfannee, ShenShen, and Boq, and the attention of debonair prince Fiyero Tigelaar.

But beneath the surface, Glinda has a big heart. Despite initially being at odds with Elphaba, she soon sees through the tough green exterior to Elphaba's vulnerable side and the two become the closest of friends.

# Glinda Upland

SHIZ UNIVERSITY
PRINCE FIYERO TIGELAAR

**"Excuse me, there's no pretense here. I happen to be genuinely self-absorbed and deeply shallow."**

***–Fiyero Tigelaar***

ROGUISH AND CAREFREE, FIYERO TIGELAAR IS THE PRINCE of Winkie Country. As the university's newest student, he quickly works to shake things up for the student population by suggesting a night at the off-limits and *scandalacious* Ozdust Ballroom.

From his first day at Shiz he shares a spark with Glinda, but it's a fateful moment in the forest outside the school where he realizes he may have much more in common with Elphaba.

# PFANNEE & SHENSHEN

Pfannee and ShenShen are Glinda's most loyal companions at Shiz. From the outset, the pair idolize Glinda for her confidence and, of course, fashion sense. Agreeing with her every word, Pfannee and ShenShen commiserate with her when she's forced to room with Elphaba, and even go so far as to conspire with her to trick Elphaba into believing the hideoteous hat sent by Glinda's gran is actually fashion forward.

The pair come to support Glinda's friendship with Elphaba, going so far as to see Elphaba off on her trip to the Emerald City.

**"It's Pfannee!"**
***–Pfannee***

**... and ShenShen!"**
***–ShenShen***

MADAME MORRIBLE

**"My personal opinion, dear, is that you do not have what it takes. I hope you prove me wrong. I doubt you will."**

***—Madame Morrible***

One of Shiz's most decorated faculty and the Dean of Sorcery Studies, Madame Morrible is the first to welcome the students to Shiz. Her magic seminars are by invitation only and held with students she herself deems worthy. Though Glinda is desperate to become a sorceress, it is Elphaba that Madame Morrible embraces after witnessing her powers in the Shiz Quad.

Madame Morrible maintains a close relationship with the Wizard, and she tells Elphaba that she may even get to meet the Wizard if she harnesses her magic. Elphaba comes to trust Madame Morrible and is finally offered the opportunity to meet the Wizard. But while Madame Morrible is supportive of Elphaba's talent, her motivations are not what they seem.

DOCTOR DILLAMOND

**"Some of us are different. And there was a time, before you were born, when life in Oz was different. When one could walk these halls and hear a snow leopard solving an equation or an antelope explicating a sonnet."**

***—Doctor Dillamond***

A WISE GOAT, DOCTOR DILLAMOND IS A HISTORY PROFESSOR and one of the last remaining animal professors left at Shiz. His class focuses on how history affects the present. As he says to his students, "The past helps explain our present circumstances."

Doctor Dillamond is aware of changes in Oz and is fearful for what it means for all of animal-kind. He confides in his fellow animal friends that he's fearful of what may happen to them. Quick to pick up his cause, Elphaba becomes an ally who understands from experience that no one should be silenced or outcast just because they're different.

SHIZ BIZ
CLUBZ & SOCIETIES
WELCOMING ALL 'SHIZMEN' TO YOUR NEW HOME AT SHIZ UNIVERSITY
KEEP
ENJOY IT CLEANLY!
YOU'RE INVITED TO SHIZ UNIVERSITY'S GARDEN SHOW
DO NOT MISS OUT!
WE WELCOME YOU TO THE DEBATABLE SOCIETY
JOIN US FOR MANY DEBATABLY ENDLESS INTELLECTUAL DISCUSSIONS
SPELLS & SORCERY
WITH THE OFFICIAL SHIZ CLUB
SHIZ CHEMISTRY CLUB
THE SHIZ QUIZ CLUB
Shiz Cycling Club
A-MAZE-IFYING CORNFIELD
A FANTABULOUS PLACE TO GET LOST AND EAT
JOIN US AT THE ARCH-ILLOGICAL FORUM
WE LOOK FORWARD TO MEETING OUR FELLOW SHIZMEN
Deadly Desertball
COME TRY-OUT AT SUNDOWN
TWISTED TORNADO TOURNAMENT
Dinkie Dancers
EXTRACURRICULAR SHIZNESS OUTSIDE OF CLASS
CLUB INFORMATION
Take Care in the Deadly Poppy Fields
DO NOT GO ALONE
SHIZ
Love to sing?
Then come join us!
CHOIR AUDITIONS
Held in the Quad
All capabilities welcome
TRY OUT TODAY!
PONG PING
DROP IN!
The Oscillationists
Questions or Queries?
ROWING CLUB
SHIZ UNIVERSITY
SOCIETY

# Student Life at

# SHIZ

Life for students at Shiz isn't always about academics. A bustling community, there's something for everyone at Shiz. Whether you're a bookworm or sports enthusiast, scholar or vocalist, Shiz has all types of extracurricular activities for its students to enjoy, including a world-class library, sports teams, choirs, a fine dining hall, or leisurely walks along its beautifical campus — all nestled against a blue lagoon.

WELCOME
TO
SHIZ

SHIZ
CHEMISTRY
CLUB

WE·WELCOME·YOU·TO
THE
DEBATABLE
SOCIETY

SHIZ

# The Ozdust Ballroom

PART 3

# The Emerald City

WELCOME
TO THE
Emerald City

WIZOMANIA
EXPERIENCE
COME
GET YOUR
TICKETS!
FOR THE MOST
SPECTACULAR
SHOW

The sights! The sounds! The Emerald City is Oz's biggest city and capital of fashion, art, and theater in the land of Oz.

Situated in the heart of Oz and just a train ride away from Shiz, the Emerald City represents opportunity and dreams come true for visitors and citizens alike. Anyone who spends time in the Emerald City is truly lucky, indeed. Home to cafés, salons, bookshops, and the hottest ticket in town, *Wizomania*, there's no shortage of things to experience in the most fantabulous—and greenest!—place in all of Oz.

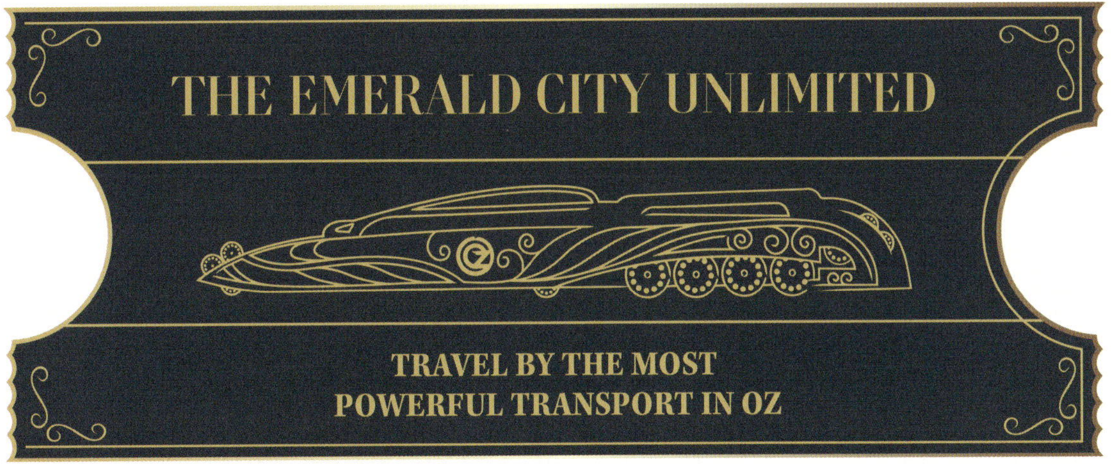
THE EMERALD CITY UNLIMITED
TRAVEL BY THE MOST
POWERFUL TRANSPORT IN OZ

W
THE WIZARD

**"Where I come from, everyone knows the best way to bring folks together is give them a real good enemy."**

***—The Wizard***

THE WIZE AND MAGNIFICENT WIZARD. THE GREAT MAGICIAN and leader of all of Oz. Though his presence is felt throughout the land, he is rarely seen. Instead, Ozians honor him through plays like *The Absotively Factual Story of the Wonderful Wizard of Oz.* The play tells the story of his arrival in Oz and his reading of the ancient book, the Grimmerie.

The Wizard grants Elphaba an audience after hearing of her abilities from Madame Morrible. At first friendly toward Elphaba and Glinda on their visit to his palace, it soon becomes clear he has ulterior motives for Elphaba and her abilities. Realizing that his policy of uniting Oz around a common enemy would unfairly hurt the animals of Oz, Elphaba becomes one of the first to challenge the Wizard.

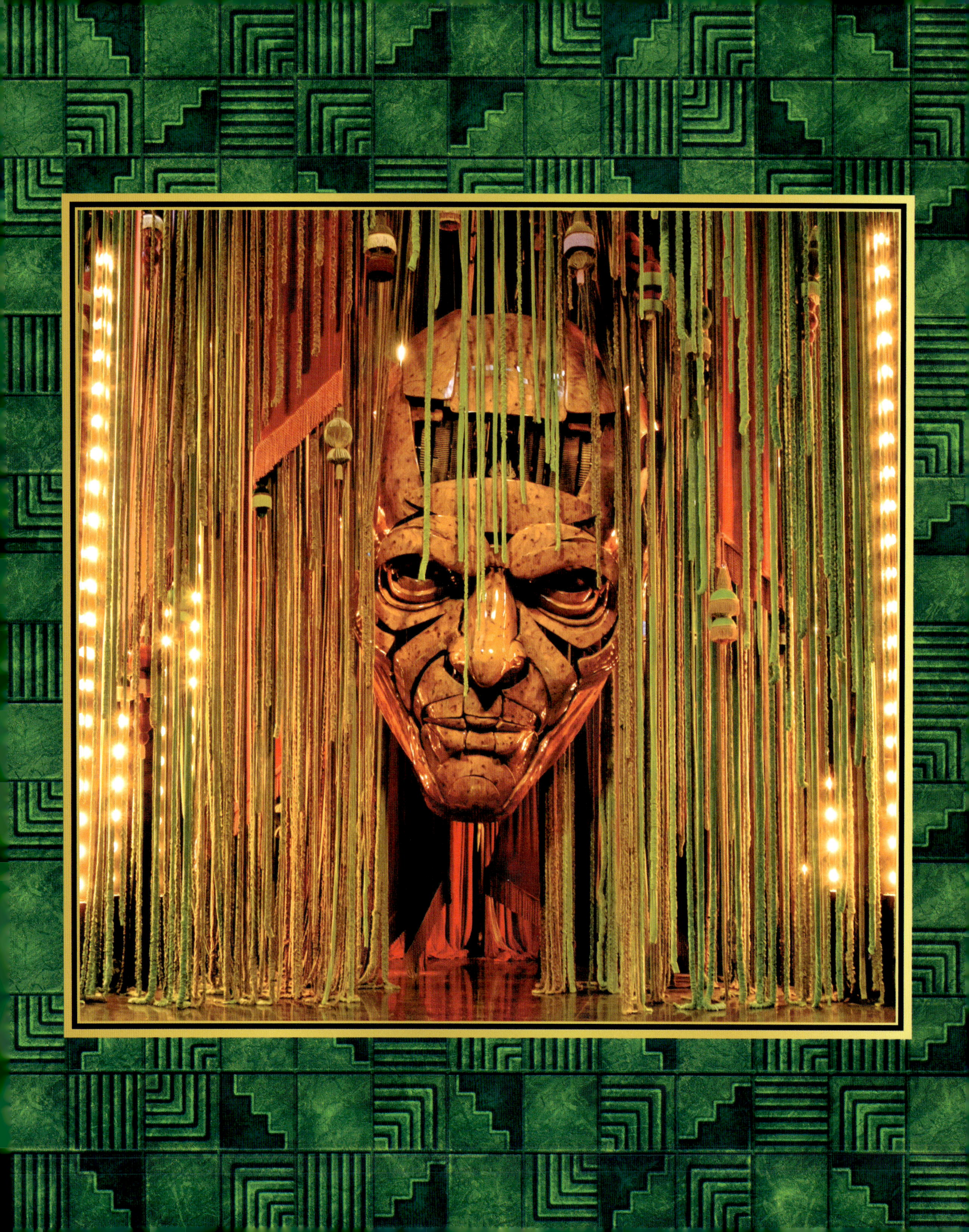

CHISTERY

Chistery is head of the Wizard's guard. When the Wizard and Madame Morrible trick Elphaba into reciting a spell from the Grimmerie, it causes him and the rest of the guards to sprout wings in a painful transformation. The Wizard intends to use Chistery and his newly formed army of flying monkeys as aerial eyes to spy on animal activity, but he first sends them to capture Elphaba after she refuses to join him in his campaign against the animals.

# Daily Life in the Emerald City

The citizens of the Emerald City enjoy all the perks of urban life. At the forefront of art, architecture, and fashion, its citizens are always coiffed and pressed in their finest emerald attire. The city has endless offerings for its citizens, including the Hot Air Café Float On In, the Emerald City Bookery, boutiques like the Emerald City Atelier, and a signature salon, the Emerald Beautification Salon. With something new around every corner it's easy to find a day's distractions along the avenues of the Emerald City.

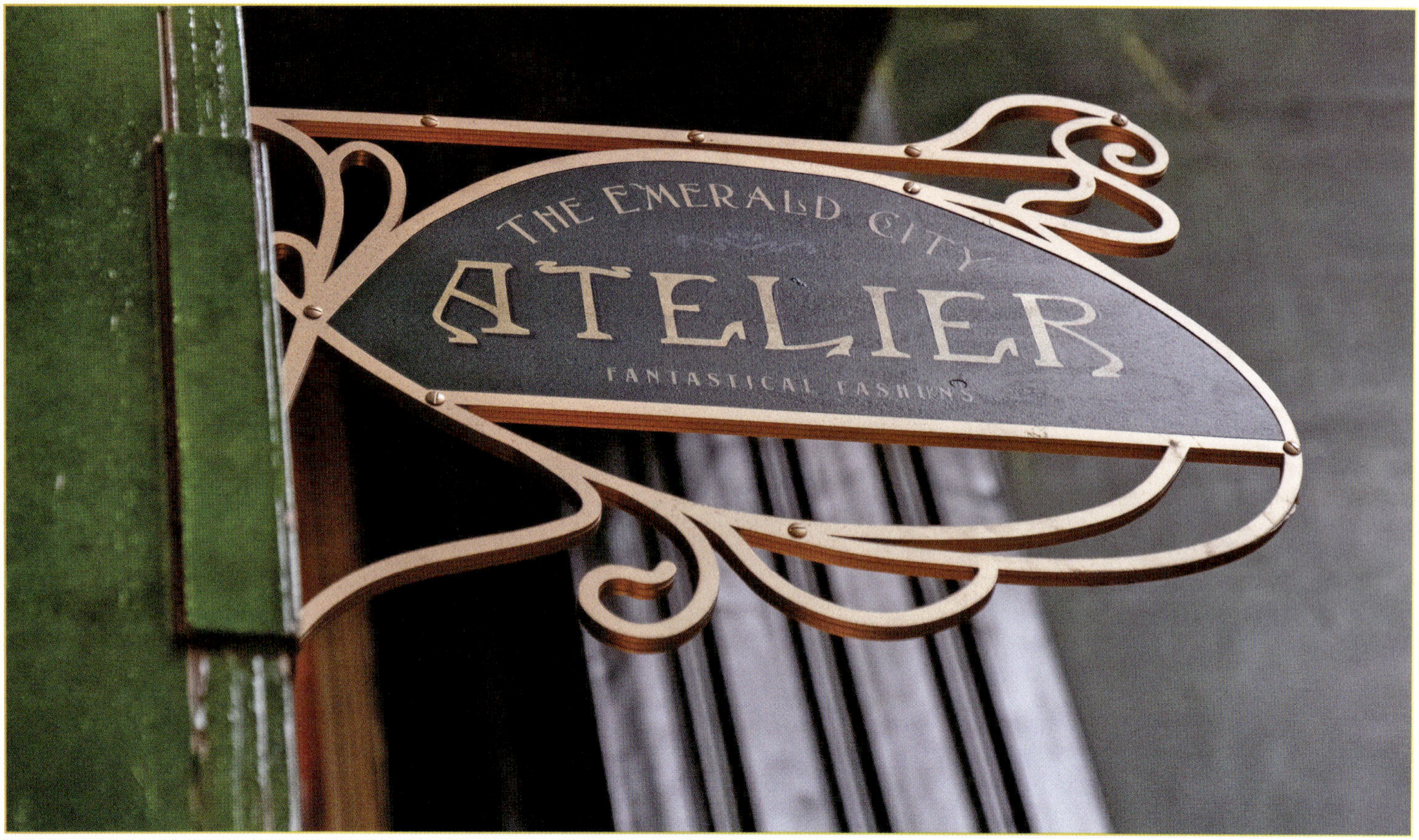
THE EMERALD CITY
ATELIER
FANTASTICAL FASHIONS

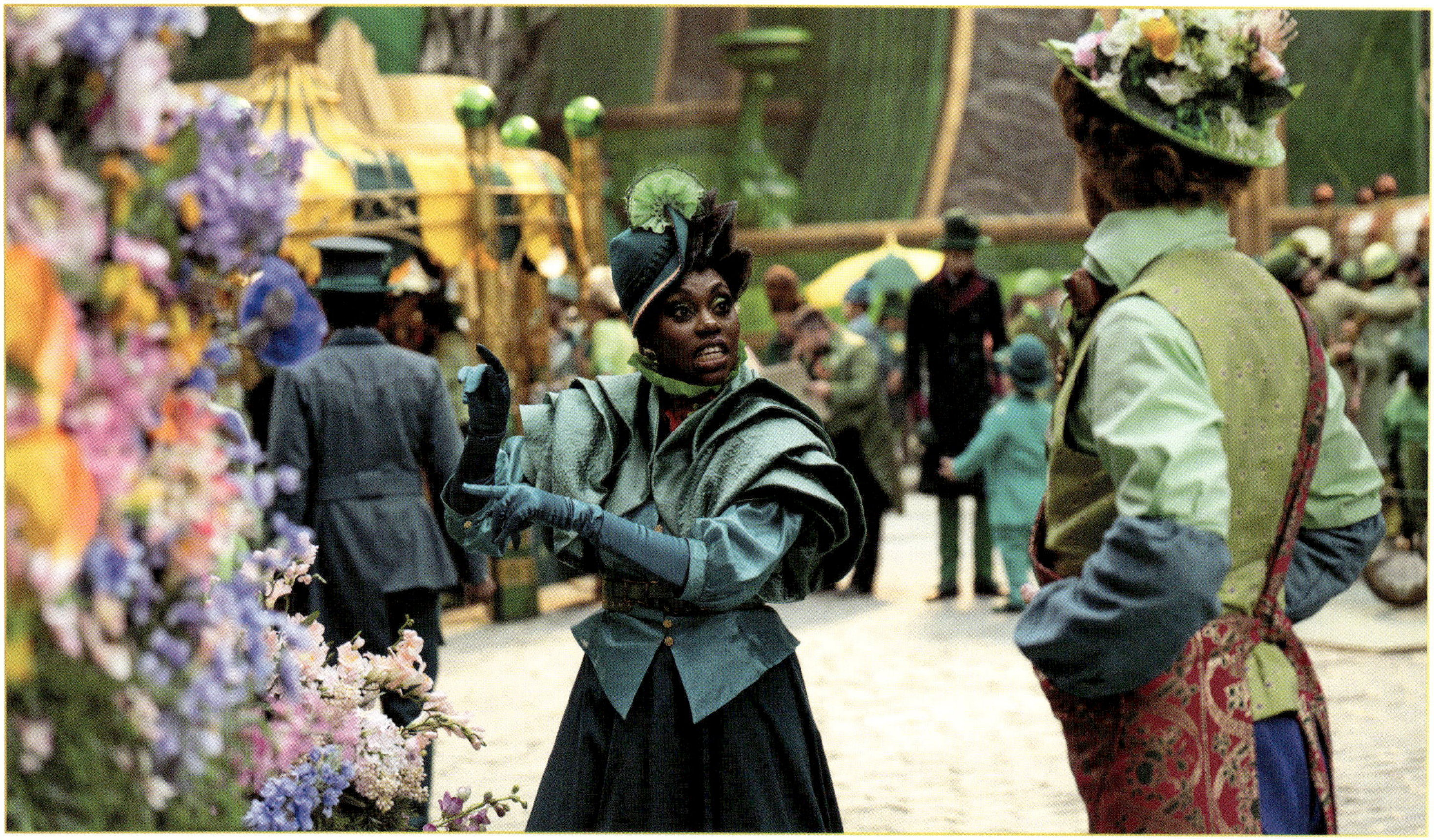

AMITY FLAIR
2ND MOON OF SPRING
Ø 80
FANCY HATS
OZMOPOLITAN
5TH MOON OF FALL
TIP
TOP
VERDE
2ND MOON OF SPRING
Ø 80
DRESS
FINESSE
NEWER THAN NEW
PAGE 5
OZMOPOLITAN
2ND MOON OF SPRING
TOP
10

WIZOMANIA

WIZOMANIA

WIZOMANIA

WIZOMANIA